AF255218

Tender Sieve

POEMS BY JOLENE NOLTE

TENDER SIEVE
Poems

Wipf & Stock
An Imprint of Wipf and Stock Publishers
199 W. 8th Ave., Suite 3
Eugene, OR 97401

www.wipfandstock.com

PAPERBACK ISBN: 978-1-6667-5879-5
HARDCOVER ISBN: 978-1-6667-5880-1
EBOOK ISBN: 978-1-6667-5881-8

Book design by Stephanie Martens

Tender Sieve

POEMS BY JOLENE NOLTE

Contents

—*To Petra*

Let everything happen to you: beauty and terror.
Just keep going. No feeling is final.

RILKE, *BOOK OF HOURS I*, 59 (TRANS. BARROWS & MACY)

Without

Without a dishwasher, I submerge
one dish at a time: blue-rimmed
cereal bowl, ribbed teal mug, wide red
colander. Fragrant water warms
my hands, warms my core.

Without a car, I move,
memorizing shades of green, tempos
of rain, the way droplets bead
on palmate and pinnate edges. I slow
my steps to remain behind the dignified
woman in periwinkle, her hair
tightly spiraled, a silver rose.

Without drywall or electricity, I watch
smoke waft from campfire ring up past
darkened hemlocks until it vanishes
into sky pricked by distant
stars, dispersed as seed.

Without lover or child, I feel
walls within me dismantle, absence
throbbing like a pulsing web just here
where blood vessels, nerve endings, and grief's
radial threads interweave. What gift
lies in this, what gift held in this tender sieve?

Desert by the Sea

The Lima Bean

Hesperia, California

Hesperia, though a desert, was still a paradise
through innocent eyes that met all barren land
with wonder. It did not occur to me that the dirt lot
lacked grass. Instead, I walked atop the stacked rows
of firewood, arms outstretched for balance—ready
at any moment for the arid wind to carry me aloft. I sang,
I danced beneath the uninhibited sky as if no one
in the world could possibly object.

That moment lima bean's slick green skin
met my tongue sent a seizure of revulsion through me.
I don't have to eat this. It wasn't so much a thought
as a tide that turned, suddenly and inexplicably.
I expelled the lima bean whole, sent it arcing
across the room, where it fell beneath the curved foot
of the wooden hutch. My mother appeared, miraculously
knew exactly what I'd done, demanded I retrieve
the bean from the shadows beneath the wood. Prostrate
on the floor in my act of penance, I noticed for the first time
the carpet was an ugly brown.

My Hesperia: An Elegy

Hesperia—a name luring defeated
Trojans to a land they'd only seen
through the gauze of hope. My Hesperia,
where I lived six years at sixteen-six-forty Ash, balancing
on the stacked rows of firewood, breathing
back lot scent of hay; where I'd sit on a wood
bench, staring at my neighbor Dorothy's wool-white hair, the opaque
swirls of her navy blue watch.

Fifteen years later, I park near the familiar corner of Ash
and E. The bench, firewood and the hay are gone.
Were they ever there? Was any element blessed
by memory actual? Hesperia
is a desert, and this
a stranger's house.

The Leap

Sixteen, at summer camp, I stood
at tower's edge in cloudless
sky-height, wooden-jointed.
I stared down at The Blob: oblong,
blue-and-yellow inflatable
bobbing on the lake below.

Others coaxed and coached,
but only I could leap. Within me
stirred a noisy council: *To jump
is to be out of control*—the thought
supplied its own evidence, visions
of broken bones. *Yes, but others
can do it, why can't I?* The tower
swayed, the lake shimmered,
The Blob continued to bob, and I
stood still.

Then rose—whence I do not know—
a decisive determination urging,
Stop rehearsing. Finally

I took a few steps back
for a running start, finally
flew off the platform, joints
and spirit consenting to bend.
My stomach rose as I plummeted,
wind roaring in my ears.
My aim was poor, feet only
skimming The Blob as I lurched
and sank into the cool lake.
No matter—I emerged new
from the encompassing blue.

Geography of Young Adulthood

Southern California

I. La Mirada

Here by morning light a coach corrected
my untutored freestyle. By moonlight, head swimming
with Plato, Pseudo-Dionysius, Dostoevsky
and mentors' guiding questions, I wound
my way beneath historic bells, past silvered olive trees.

Here I learned to lay myself bare, to let
a midwife of the soul see and speak
into the labor of becoming.

II. Los Angeles

That night I picked up my roommate
from LAX, I spent an hour, maybe two, inching,
inching up Century Boulevard—
Mozart on my radio—while she circled.
By the time authorities gave the all clear,
all was backlogged—patience

threadbare, car horns blaring.
I parked in the terminal lot, found
her, loaded her luggage when
the thong of my right sandal
snapped.

III. Huntington Beach

My cousins and I huddled by the bonfire, watched
moonbeams diffuse on the Pacific and the couple
just ahead of us, their arms encircling
one another's waists. *That will soon be me.*

A decade later, I bid this place goodbye. Tonight
moonbeams ripple beyond the firelight. My waist
remains untouched.

IV. Cypress

An indistinct city poorly named: Monterey cypress limbs extend
as weathervanes on seaside crags, but these do not grow
in this suburban soil. Nor does the city have anything to do
with the ancient Mediterranean island.
This town's namesake looks like overgrown
fingers stretched skywards. I lived there simply because it lay
halfway between my roommate's workplace and mine.
So for six years we called Cypress home.

At night it offered us the sight of refracted
light from the complex pool dancing
on fig leaves overhead, while our neighbor
watered his jasmine, singing.

Pacific Theophany

Once on the Pacific, just offshore,
I saw the marine gray ridge
of a blue whale's spine, showing but one brief
section at a time as it arced slowly
downward to dive as if the invisible rotation
of a gargantuan wheel. An indented plateau finally
appeared, and as a parting gift, the krill-nourished
giant revealed its full fluke. The world's largest animal
in history—sublimity beckoning in what I had
and hadn't seen, that slivered backside, that glimpse of glory,

Opa at Home

Alta Loma, California. In memory of my paternal grandfather.

One last time he inhaled, air rasping through his crowded
corridors to his failing lungs, his head and renegade strand
of hair jerked in the effort. Then—silence, stillness, head
bowed like a child's, asleep at last in the car seat.
Four years' battle ended there in the thick-knit fabric
of his favorite chair, there with three generations
to feel one last time the thickness, the weight
of his sun-speckled hands.

Oma and Opa's Garden

The spheres sang—bright
lemons and oranges, creamy
yellow pomelos, tangerines
and cumquats. We ran
from tree to tree while Birds
of Paradise looked on.
We gathered pastel eggs, joined
the chorus of color with squeals
of laughter in our Easter best.

+

Even as a child, I took issue
with the forbidden fruit's
being an apple. What could be
so tempting about so common a crop?

Oma and Opa's garden
held no apples.

+

The day of Opa's funeral, we posed
for family photos beneath the avocado trees.
Sunlight cascaded in golden shafts
down San Gabriel granite to where we stood,
bewildered in our mourners' black.

+

And now, Oma and I linger over breakfast, her garden
visible through lace curtains. I am thirty-one, still
without the usual accouterments (husband, house,
children, preferably in that order). She forgets my age,
has no notion that her words are barbed. *Thirty-one?*
You'd better hurry; Thirty-one? When I was your age,

I had three kids toddling around. Though I try to tell her
that she presses on a deep, an open wound, she does not
know what she does. At eighty-seven, with sun spots
and wearing both her and Opa's
wedding bands on her arthritic hands, still
she keeps the garden, to which I escape for quiet.

Lemons, oranges, avocados, pomelos still shine,
as orbs of transformed sunlight. When did love
and lack of love become so intertwined?
When did family become an echo chamber
of loneliness from which our branching paths divide?

I stand a bit straighter, but my new blouse
does not dress the wound. This garden is smaller
than I remembered. Birds of Paradise with their sharp
blue plumes tell me the way back is barred.
I do not know if I will see this garden again.

Pentecost

After my maternal grandmother's passing, Walnut, California.

As a mother of nine children, what were a few more?
When she babysat in the sixties, *Mrs. Ortega* became
'Tega on a toddler's tongue, then on her children's.
Thereafter we called her nothing else.

In 2016, we knew 'Tega's tongue gave her trouble, how its swelling
pain garbled her speech, made even yogurt difficult
to eat. We never imagined it was spreading its poison
through her, making irrevocable claim on her just after doctors
finally correlated symptoms to their accurate, icy name: cancer.

Her funeral had to wait an extra week because of Pentecost,
a high holiday at San Lorenzo. Under the trellis-topped gazebo,
under the gray chill of an overcast morning, under the weight
of fresh grief, we—a dozen of her progeny—sat as guests
in her honor, beneath the red and yellow fabric waves, woven,
this year as every year, into the gazebo ceiling above.

Before the mass began, her lighthearted priest told us
what we already knew: how she had helped to found this place,
how she guarded the donuts with vigilance, and lately labored
to speak. Yet the warmth with which he spoke of her offered
some comfort.

Clouds of incense warmed the damp air. The day's reading
swelled into a linguistic stereo as parishioners at every corner told
of the Spirit's fiery descent, each in their mother tongue.

Tongue-tip to the back of my teeth, *Thanks*
demanded conscious effort as I thought of 'Tega, her loss
of ability to articulate. Still, the Word of the Lord
pronounced here, many-tongued.

"Thanks be to God."

Pacific Migration

Freeways and theme parks swarmed
as a beehive, heatwaves from the golden,
gauzy light radiating from concrete, blurring
the edges of the eye. Azaleas, bougainvillea,
eucalyptus grew, oranges and lemons too, but I
watched for the seeds I planted hoping
they'd break through our caked soil. No single

stem appeared. My linoleum floor might
at any time give way. Nor could I be sure
my bedframe would hold—being, as it was,
a makeshift raft adrift. In the moments
between sleeping and waking, I saw
myself lost—a fragile island in the ocean.

Thereafter, I followed gray whale mothers
guiding their calves north, along gray shores
where lichen clings to fir and alder, slick
with rain, and barnacles grip tight to whale skin.

Wine-Dark Tides

i.
Some days I deem myself
victim of God's neglect.

Forgetful God, remember
me, who never
asked to be.
     Just now,
with blood stuttering
from heart to artery to capillary
to vein, only to return to the core
I ask, *Why give me such*
ebbing and flowing
intricacies to sustain
my being
only to let me feel all
as emptiness?

I ask, *Why beset me*
with desire and not supply
fulfillment?

ii.
And yet my body
enacts more hope
than my mind
can muster. I choose
not to make my bed
because I know the binding sheets
will soon serve to bear the body
into sleep's shadow-realm.

In the dark
hollow within me, mindless,
my body continues
to prepare the primordial
nursery. Never mind
that this body knows nothing
but waiting; the innate
custodian gathers the unused
sheets. As ever, she will return
to make up the bed
again. I see no reason
this time could not be different.

Unseen Stipe

Pedestrian

Vancouver, BC

At the open coffee shop window,
I stare out blankly at squat
buildings, one painted turquoise,
and distant glass skyscrapers rising
beneath the Coast Mountains' jagged
ears. *Living Poetically* sits on the table
beside my iced coffee; my thoughts
flit like sparrows in June sky. What relation
bides between word and world, substance
and spirit? How might they unite
in the movement of a life?

On the sidewalk a tan man carries
two potted palms crisscrossed
against his chest. The fronds extend,
leafy wings jostling as he walks—Pegasus
come down from Parnassus. Given a gust
of wind, just imagine how he'd fly—
above cars, discarded cups, and every concrete
edifice—drawing all perceiving eyes his way.

As So Much Fluff

Floating, ascending, slow-drifting
cottonwood seedclouds circle
very like a warm snowstorm, or daytime
constellation, or roving host
in sky's ample apse.

From my periphery they bloom to fill
my vision where I lie face to the sky
in backyard grass, entranced. O
to be a wisp of fluff ablaze, aloft
in a shaft of late May sun! I'd know nothing
but light, air, and ease—though one tuft
I'd be a multitude, still free, though earthborn,
earthbound, flying still.

Cyclamen

(after Rilke)

Five-petalled magenta—halfway
between royal blue and blood red—poised,
an umbrella blown inside out. Each stem
dives forward while petal-wings stretch back.

As an osprey trembles midair, then folds
its wings to rocket down, so these flowers
throw open, propelled center-first.

Picasso's *Maternidad* at the Doctor's Office

Maternity becomes her, softening,
as it does, her whole body, now
in full flower, her skin cherry-
blossom pink and white.
Her chest exposed, her clavicle
diagonal as she cranes neck and head
rightward, down to feast upon the radiance
of her baby's face—she remains a vision
to which Picasso and I are common strangers.

I'm told motherhood is not so rosy.
It's almost animal, a friend confided,
her baby smacking loudly at her breast.
A clogged duct in her nipple sent her
to the hospital. *You're always
breastfeeding,* another new mom
relates, *and it's unrelenting.*

Still I sit, a patient on tissue-thin
paper, waiting, reflexively weeping
before *Maternidad.* Chill air sweeps
through my open-backed gown, shrivels
my untouched breasts. I shiver
at the blithe abyss, vertiginous,
between maternity and me.

Morning

When I rise and find nothing new in my phone's blue glow, I taste something of death—the earth makes its rounds apart from me.

When I step outside, greeted by a host of fragrant green, I taste something of life—this swirling world beckons me to savor and see.

On Visiting the Loretto Chapel Staircase

Santa Fe, New Mexico

I lay awake last night, and lay awake
the night before, and also the night before that
in my sister's guest room, while my sister
slept beside her husband, their two boys
having finally succumbed to sleep, snug
in beds cluttered with stuffed animals. I still
am turning over impossibilities: How
do I—a woman ever alone atop the mattress—believe
in the darkness that I am wanted, loved?
O you who have kept count of my tossings, put my tears
in your bottle, why count rather than remove?

Today I enter the Loretto Chapel—unlikely
Gothic eminence embodied here among arroyos,
piñon, and sage. Unbending stone extends
vaulted above, heaven's ribs borrowed
to form this ceiling of heaven, these
scarlet and sapphire shafts reaching
through stained glass, these walls
of suffering, stations of the cross. At the center,
at the crux of crucifix and altar, death
becomes life, and eternity cups time.

A wooden staircase spirals without central
column. Somehow it holds. No one knows
the carpenter's name. He disappeared,
left his impossible staircase for the choir
to ascend. Now rough rope and a sign
bar me from mounting those miraculously
wound steps. So I sit at its base, wondering,
Why is it that your wounds should feed me? Why
have you given me not only the breath

but even the words with which I accuse,
lament, and complain to you?

My temples throb from lack of sleep
as I depart the chapel and witness anew
the deep July blue sky, the moths that hover
like hummingbirds, these turquoise doors
in red adobe walls, and hear the music
of my name in my nephew's voice.

Later, in another arid night, as my head falls again
onto the pillow of a borrowed room, the impossible
staircase spirals in my mind's eye. And, yes, the familiar
ache of longing pricks the breastbone's channel, swells
within my ribcage walls. Through the open window, piñon
perfumes the room. In darkness, those same trees wait
beside our narrow, dry arroyo, ready to receive
whatever waters the heavens might provide.

The Rift

The nothing that is everything
stretches indeterminately.

Raw ache rivers down my throat, cleaves
my ribcage, then scars and craters my core.

How do I yet hold together?
What am I held together for?

Swimming backstroke over the deep
end, my sides alternately tilt.

Unease subsides as I'm steadied
by my rift, this column of breath, proceeding.

Concert A

Smell of resin and my musty
clarinet case, my reed's wood taste
on my tongue as I assemble
my inherited instrument:
mouthpiece, barrel, body joints, bell.
Behind me, brass section's spittle
bubbles, spills in staccato *pffts!*
A cacophony of phrases,
scales, arpeggios swirl in C
major, F sharp, B flat minor—
until the white baton's light taps
command our sudden stillness.

With a cue, the concertmaster
at the conductor's side sounds A,
the one note to which our many
warm dark bright airy timbres tune.

Variation on the Void

for though I claw at empty air and feel
nothing, no embrace,
I have not plummeted
—"Suspended" by Denise Levertov

I, too, suspect a void where I am upheld
in the darkness, though the abyss,
even so, threatens to swallow me.

We read of black holes, of the cold
enormity of space, of the deserts
within the particles we imagined
were packed like a box of marbles—
is all this emptiness our nightmare
brooding atop a chaos of waters?

The Spirit hovers over the void, carves
out pathways. Occasionally we might
dare move our feet and find ourselves yet
supported, conscious we have unfathomable
depths to fall. We falter, only to feel a warm
grip—firm, steadying beneath our arms, invisibly,
invariably, ever upholding.

Paradox of Flight

Low tide at Spanish Banks, a lone gull swoops
low, its light and hollow frame nearly wingtip
to wingtip with its transitory double.

Then it descends into the still tidal pool, mounts
invisible currents upward—tethered
together by an unseen stipe.

Prophetic Sight

To hear
the bleating sheep,

to see Agag, bound
but breathing, and to read

fear in the face
of broad-shouldered Saul.

To speak
words to dethrone the cowardly,

to walk away, leaving
the poor offerings unlit.

To heed
the Voice that pierces hearts,

to touch with the oil
of anointing the shepherd boy's

fleece-black curls, his open
glistening face.

End of August

Look. Witness the touch
of seraphim coal visible
on us, enriching each maple, birch,
sunburst honey locust, ornamental
pear trees' leaves turning gold, crimson,
vermillion, in clusters.

Though spring's soft drizzle
and summer's unveiled sun
nourished us, we find ourselves
unloosed by autumn's azure
breath. We return to the ground, where
our blazing colors dwindle to earth
tones. Winter's slosh and booted feet
assist our dissolution.

Regardless, we stand august
now because we trust
this unquenchable
fire will bear us, yes,
deep into cold clay, but—Lord
knows how—one day up
again to greet the sapphire sky.

Winter Evening Ritual

Wander the neighborhood, and note
the beads clinging to leaf tips, glistening
in streetlamp-light. Feel cold air pressing
your face in the thick dark, passing
through your coat, through even the skin's
membrane—a chilling bloom
entering the thighs quietly, exponentially
until it envelopes even your femur.

Strange, the cure for permeating
cold: Submerge hands and forearms
in hot dishwater. Let its bubbling
warmth pervade invisibly, from arms
to core to thighs to toes. Lay dishes
to dry and cast the day's chill words
aside like so many stones.

Long Echo

*Out there in the silence [she]
makes everything echo [her] pain,
and this echo of pain is the poem.*

SØREN KIERKEGAARD

For P

If he sees these pages, she'd have him know
that she grants him his freedom. Or, rather,
she accepts what freedom was always his,

like that of eagles kiting high over
Pacific Spirit Park. His spirit, from
the first time they met, recalled to her mind

those keen-eyed, matchless birds. Now that he's flown
to where she cannot follow, she accedes
to his silence.

She Cries, Part 1

He is kind to her and very pretty.
He's bright, he writes, he's cultured and artsy,
but most of all, he makes her feel so seen.
Perhaps at last, her ideal's not a dream!

She knows he has his own mind, volition,
yet she falls hard, despite her suspicion
that he abides ballparks out of her league.
He remains aloof, a man of intrigue.

They exchange work, words of affirmation—
he says he enjoys their conversation.
Nothing more happens. For him, it's simply
(apparently) writerly repartee.

Then he tells her that he's juggling too much.
One last exchange, then he falls out of touch.
He lives just a kilometer from her,
but for months, they do not see each other.

She cries on the bus; she cries in the hall;
she cries in the stacks, the bathroom stall.
She subsists on coffee; her pants don't fit.
She swims for solace, leaves her hair wet.

She tries to cope. She gets help; leaves him be.
But she nurses her pain into misery,
its food the story she constructs, recites
to herself throughout her days and nights.

Her every, long-held insecurity
and her dearth of romantic history
form "proof" she trusts unequivocally:
physically, metaphysically

there is something wanting and very wrong—
she has suspected as much all along.

Awake

Even in shorts and a tee, he seemed
a vision. Once, per her request,
just the two of them met for (his request)
just a half-hour. (She read his cue.)

In a coffee shop named for a Whitman poem,
he sat across the table from just her,
the sun lighting his (divine) curls, (dreamy)
green eyes, chin narrow (so well-proportioned)
as he holds, focused, silent, listening to her.

He cradles his red mug of steaming
green tea, smiling. (What perfection!)
When he held her writing between
his slender fingers, told her what
he saw there, she felt flush
for days thereafter.

She'd never liked herself more
than when he said these things
as he looked right at her.

What does he think of her?
She subsequently scrutinizes this scene
for clues in dark hours, even weeks,
(yes—months) thereafter,
though she knows this a futile
(juvenile) line of inquiry.

She never disliked herself more
than when she deemed herself *infinitely
insufficient* to hold his interest.

April Dusk at the Camosun Bog

Pacific Spirit Park, BC

Though their convergence was brief,
he had become both her Virgil and Beatrice,
so when he left, he left her both reduced
and increased by that searing hole, his absence.
(Yes, her disappointment tends towards the hyperbolic.)

But just now, she's no pilgrim pressing ahead.
Back in the forest, April in the Camosun Bog,
the blackberries he loves are a dream waiting
to be roused. Dusky sky and hemlocks pool,
mirrored in the standing water.

She has become porous in these waterlogged
months without a glimpse of him. (Her every coat
pocket holds a foundation-smeared tissue.
Even she can smirk at this.) Like sphagnum moss,
thin-membraned with strange powers of preservation,
she keeps his words—and his silence—within her.
Sphagnum grows above its own decaying layers.

Still, the bog's hemlock-rimmed depression
enables heaven's reflection. Falling for him
taught her how love rends one's Being open—
embraces not just the fruit but suffers
the wait, the thorn, the stain.

Good Friday 2019

His silence pierces her (or so she
tells herself, being of late
given to melodrama. See above.)

An eviscerated shade (see?), she walks through
morning fog, receives
it as a garment, as a shroud.

      Eight years old on Good Friday night,
      fearful of her flu—her body retching,
      rejecting its contents, trailing that awful
      acidic taste—she heard her brother say,
      "If you feel this way, imagine
      how Jesus felt."

      Some comfort, she thought, as she cradled
      the beige bucket. *At least Sprite
      is better than vinegar.* But her terror
      took a new texture:

      If God did not let Jesus escape, if Jesus
      who is God does not avoid but writhes
      in pain, what hope does any have for reprieve?

Fog lifts by afternoon, by evening it is Christ's flesh she eats—
flesh of her speared Lord, who in reckless love exposed
himself. More harrowing than his cry of agony,
the God-forsaken silence.

She has tasted but a crumb of Love's wretchedness.

At Ruckle Park Campground

Salt Spring Island, BC

I. Dialogue at Dawn

Conscious of her bladder and birdsong,
she lumbers to the nearby outhouse
with neither her glasses nor her flashlight.
Before returning to her tent, she ambles
down the seaside path, discerns
the blurred crescent moon spilling
its glowing cordial on the bay
while dawn begins to ripen, peach.

He'd love this place. She sighs. Why does he *still*
matter to her? Unbeckoned, his words to her
from last July reverberate: "I tend
to think of life as an adventure."
Her reply: "I like that." She still does.
Who wouldn't? There's a reason why
clichés are cliché. No? Heedless, he's not
here where night dovetails to day—salt sea
encircled by islands just now rousing from sleep.

She hears phrases of birds' matins blending
in cadenced wash and backwash of waves. Even
bleary-eyed at the bay's border, she witnesses
the tête-à-tête of fading moonlight, the keen
solidity of dawn. Just now, that familiar ache
in her throat softens, and just for a moment
that weary loneliness wanes to solace, even
tastes sweet.

II. Jupiter Ascendant

Gulf Islands' fir-crested ridges puncture the sky, bleed it
of day's vibrancy until only languishing blue remains.

A single star appears: *Jupiter*, the woman at the common
campfire tells her. She recalls how last summer she lent him *Ballistics:*

He returned it promptly through a friend who relayed,
"He said to tell you his favorite was the one about Jupiter."

Now, despite her vigilance and his rebuffing distance, he again
has risen with that faraway helium giant, chief among her thoughts.

Doesn't he know that even six hundred million miles cannot erase
but only punctuate his traces in a silent, beleaguered sky?

And she? Does she not know how little such thoughts
figure in the object she observes?

She Cries, Part 2

On the third floor at the edge of Point Grey
she sits with ten disciples every Friday.
They practice letting their attention rest
on the continuous movement of breath.

Her thoughts are clouds drifting by, but she grows
in returning to her breath's ebb and flow.
Outside gulls cry, construction buzzes, beeps;
They all sit straight, eyes closed, breathing. She weeps.

They acknowledge their own pain, and—how strange
—it helps them accept all they cannot change.
She can't change his mind, but she sure can cry.
These tears for her self-inflicted injury

yield gradually to tears of simple grief.
She meets her judgments with some disbelief,
recognizes the ways she elevates
him but herself she underestimates,

concluding her fate's a lonely doom.
The thoughts pass; she feels her feet in the room,
shifts her attention back to her breath's rush
to her abdomen, the way her own sides brush

and fall away from her sweater's softness.
The bell's ring wakes her to outer world's largeness.
She doesn't mind that the others can see
streaks on her cheeks. Grief's shared transparency

is better than lonely obscurity.
She leaves lighter, walks to the bus—freshly
aware of earth beneath her feet, of sound,
of breath within her, its steadying ground.

Various Addresses

A Note to Doomsday Calculators

The Lord suggests we not predict the day and the hour,
but as you persist in this, at least remember: First,
it's not the doom of a cosmic detonation so much as
the rending of a curtain at the cellular and celestial
levels—a dazzling advent that, yes, burns
and blinds like fire, but most essentially
transforms like light.

Second, if you must bet on chronology, put your money
on a Sunday. This really ought to govern your calculations,
for Sunday is the day when the ribcage of space expands
while time holds its breath, when fasts
may be broken while bread and wine present
body and blood, when Death first felt defeat
while *Theanthropos* quit the open tomb at dawn.

Much remained unchanged: Rome still ruled, fishermen kept
fishing, scribes scribing; there was and is still marrying
and burying, buying and selling. Even so, the world was renewed
that morning: eyes opening, hearts burning, feet running, breath
forgotten then quickened as the scarred, resurrected Lord appeared.
What to make of it?—more fruitful mystery? So,
who's to say his return won't be on a Sunday?

One Sunday

Scent of dry earth, rosemary, and salt-
kissed air that Sunday at Torrey Pines. Atop
the chalky cliff, I held you, Peter, on my hip,
your head by my shoulder as we watched sunlight
spark across the ever-shifting
Pacific plain.

You'd just turned one the day before. Already
you'd nearly outgrown your white
sun hat, but your sight
not yet precise enough to grasp,
to recognize the geyser of vapor emerging
from a solid curve amongst the waves. I gasped,
pointed, "Look, a whale! A gray."

I hope you remember, somewhere
in the deep recess upon which our lives
yet float, such sheer blessedness that day.

To the UBC Aquatic Centre
Women's Locker Room

I have never seen myself in three dimensions all in one glance.
That comprehensive view has been granted to you.

Once in middle school, girls in another locker room laughed
at my Latina ass. But now I am here where I change into my suit
as I hear one woman tutor another on the trick of the locker:
"Hold the handle up the *whole time*, put the coin in, close it,
and *then* turn the key." When I turn around, I see the speaker's
stark naked, buxom buttocks and all.

Undergraduate students vent in righteous indignation
on themes of feminism and inclusion. One among them, like me,
has faint acne scars on her back, no less beautiful for that.

Morning regulars include a woman with jet-black hair
and brown-sugar skin, early 40s; and another, silver-haired
with sun-speckled complexion, mid 70s, both similar
to my short height, small cup size. I aspire to be like them,
comfortable in their own warm-toned skin, still swimming.

Every so often an exhibitionist leaves off clothes for a while,
affording even respectful, averting eyes a chance to see
organic female glory

After my post-swim shower, I return to my locker,
dab on and rub in lavender lotion, aware
that this process leaves me open to view.
So be it. I've accepted, thanks to all of you, I
am a real woman, too.

To Keats

inspired by Keats Hall, UBC

In this autumnal universe, Mr. Keats, a building
bears your name. Perhaps you'd be pleased to see
it lies adjacent to Chaucer Hall, but especially that
it's bordered by a glimmering galaxy
of sweet gum trees. Across the street
lies a hospital. Perhaps these bright
stars are not steadfast, but, like you,
brilliant to the dying breath.

Five-pointed leaves form a cosmos of yellow,
red, purple, and green. They are exploding
in ecstatic excess of light, paving the ground
in golden debris before winter's impending darkness.

This leaf, for instance, is deep crimson at its slender tips,
ocher at its center. Will the purpled dark
overwhelm the center like an imploding star?

A Valentine to the *Font* Figure

(in the Regent College library sculpture by David Robinson)

Come off the world's edge with me now—
or, at least, scoot over. We'll find room
for me to help you shoulder these twin weights
of body and spirit, possibility and necessity.
Balance is precarious, I know. I too exist apart.
Yet the sphere of human being admits
some company, some comfort in solidarity.
Let me share your point of view.

We may slip, topple over, but then we'd discover
together water we can wade, follow to a new
shore whose Saturn-like meniscus ends
where a world of inquiry begins. What if
you joined me in reality's rush—breath
and bread, flesh and blood? Or what if
you stayed, alone, perfectly poised
in oxidized obsidian?

Desiring the Moon

i.
To see the moon, forget
easy illustrations, a fingernail
crescent. Look, not simply
for the glowing sliver, but also
the subtle outline of a sphere.

To see the beloved, forget
stock plotlines where love
is always eventually requited.
Look beyond your own pining
to the wide night sky:

Consider the moon as it also
spins in space, drawing
tides, stealing your breath
while keeping its own
elliptical course. Remember
no one can capture the moon.

ii.
The trouble's not so much
desiring but grasping.
As with forbidden fruit,
that luminous sphere remains
a bright, created good;
it is we who are ill-prepared
to metabolize the potent nectar.

Single Life

i.
Line up the days in rows; leave
space between them.
Guard those spaces from weeds
and rabbits and slugs. Watch
that the herbs do not flower
and embitter the green bounty.
Give peas a trellis, or else find
their vines entangled, clinging
to stalk and branch and leaf.
Pick off anything withered; watch
where the light you cannot summon falls
across the hours and the seasons.
Welcome the rainwater, the way it accentuates
every scent.

ii.
Mary was drawing water
for her garden when Gabriel
appeared. She dropped
her pitcher, and her knees
buckled, hit the ground, where
at first her eyes sought refuge
from the penetrating light. A voice
like many waters called
her name. "Do not be afraid."
Then the famous announcement:
Allow the Holy Spirit to enter
the recess within you and there
plant a seed you will bear, deliver,
for a time you will tend. This fruit
will save. *Let it be unto me, just so.*

She could not have imagined
how these words, the precious
seed in her womb would open
her to such a wound as would come.

iii.
Offer your emptiness. Do not
fear tears. Joined by light and by another's
hidden Presence, you cannot predict
what such harrowing will yield.

iv.
When you find such weeds,
as these, do not rush
to yank them. First, sit
among them as would attend
the Lover of your soul. Meet
his gaze even there, and see
how he does not define you
by dandelion or ragweed,
but looks to witness his life
uniquely brought to bear
in you.

v.
If a woman wears
a dress in a room alone,
is she still beautiful?

If a woman stretches
across her bed alone, are the curves
of her body still lovely?

If she has never
received a seed, will she yet
bear fruit?

If she never draws
an infant mouth to her
breast, what will be her legacy?

When she ponders
these things in her heart
by moonlight, do you hear her?

When she offers
you these aching, fallow
spaces, what will you plant?

In Memory of 'Tega
(*for my maternal grandmother*)

Nowhere does your pool contain
Mediterranean blue. But it's that vibrant hue
that re-immerses me: Mary's color

like the upturned bowl of sky
where strata of our biosphere overlay
occasioning an incomprehensible depth
of blue. As if that sapphire propels
the body skyward, waits
to receive, to bless when awe swells
throat and chest. As if the azure dome
is our own to swim, unending
as a summer day. All that glory,
world without end.

                I've never seen your hair so white
                as when I enter your room to say goodbye.
                I cross over to your bed, where your rosary dangles
                beside you. Your skin seems merely
                a membrane draping your bones, your gaunt
                fingers interlace with mine. *Preserve us,*
                Mother, now and at the hour of our death.

Childhood summers, I felt the world alive, myself awake
in your backyard—on the other side of your bedroom wall—
where the aqua slide would plunge me into the deep.
Chlorine stinging my nostrils, water's weight
pressing in on my ears, I grasp how easily
the light-streaked depth could overpower me.

Your ring fits me. Opal's blue cast,
iridescent streaks remind me of you
and of those free, endless-seeming days.

Ache and awe still well up within me
at the sight of a high summer sky, under which
I am forever splashing in your pool with my mates.
You look on from a chair in the sun, wearing
your rosary, smiling in your somber delight.

My aunts and I pack up glassware I never saw
you use: milky hobnail vase, translucent
serving bowls—remnants of a life—
and we the fruit of your womb. For us all,
childhood's gone. Summer
comes. Your house sells.

In the wake of that
deep, living blue—
all that glory—even so
as it was in the beginning,
        is now, and ever
shall be world without end

Consolations

When you welcome the stray
cat's approach across the empty
street to your outstretched hand
and linger as it lets you stroke
its circling length . . .

When you offer the ache,
and let fall the dammed
flow of tears . . .

When you receive another's affirming
words as winged seeds unfolding,
fluttering down to inarticulate depths . . .

When you feel yourself enfolded
by summer's breath
that bends golden grasses, transforms
ponderosas' silence to ocean waves . . .

When you discover, though your blistered,
bloodied hands can no longer grip the oars,
the current has carried you to an undiscovered,
fragrant, fir-lined shore.

ACKNOWLEDGMENTS

Thank you to the Regent community, my Vancouver writing groups, my friends, family, and previous teachers for your support at various stages. This collection would not be possible without you. Particular thanks to Scott Cairns for the feedback on earlier drafts of these poems. Special thanks to Diane Tucker, who first suggested that I seek publication, and to Petra Anderson for exhorting me to pursue poetry as a matter of spiritual significance. I am deeply grateful to my family and to Regula and Alice for helping to make the presentation of this work in its creative thesis stage such a beautiful occasion. Thanks as well to Steph Martens for your excellent work on the design. Thanks to Emily for years of persistent friendship. Last but not least, thanks to David for encouraging me to take the next step.

Thanks as well to the editors of the following for publishing previous versions of these poems:

BORROWED SOLACE	"My Hesperia: An Elegy," "Pacific Migration"
CRUX	"End of August," "Prophetic Sight"
CURATOR	"Concert A"
EKSTASIS	"Morning," "The Rift"
ET CETERA	"A Valentine to the Font Figure," "Cyclamen," "The Leap," "To Keats," "Winter Evening Ritual"
FATHOM MAGAZINE	"Oma and Opa's Garden," "One Sunday," "Pacific Theophany," "Single Life," "Wine-Dark Tides"
PENSIVE	"To the Aquatic Centre Women's Locker Room"
PQ REVIEW	"Picasso's *Maternidad* at the Doctor's Office"
RED ROCK REVIEW	"Opa at Home"

These poems explore the relationship between inner and outer worlds. They are both the record of the search and the means of searching, whether it's on a walk, witnessing a relative's death, experiencing unrequited love, or simply waking up and washing dishes. Laced with longing as well as delight, Tender Sieve explores both the grief and joy of finding a way forward when life doesn't look like you expected.

ABOUT THE AUTHOR

Jolene Nolte currently lives in Vancouver, British Columbia where she enjoys the innumerable shades of green and where she studied theology and poetry at Regent College (MATS). She works as a freelance writer and editor.